THE EUGÉNIE ROCHEROLLE SERIES

Intermediate Piano Solo

Romantic Stylings

8 Original Piano Solos by Eugénie Rocherolle

2	Café de Paris
8	Celebración
5	Last Dance
16	Longings
12	Memento
22	Rapsodie
19	Reflections
28	Romance

On the cover:
Bal du moulin de la Galette, 1876
by Pierre-Auguste Renoir (1841–1919)

ISBN 978-1-5400-6168-3

HAL•LEONARD®

Visit Hal Leonard Online at
www.halleonard.com

Contact us:
Hal Leonard
7777 West Bluemound Road
Milwaukee, WI 53213
Email: info@halleonard.com

In Europe, contact:
Hal Leonard Europe Limited
42 Wigmore Street
Marylebone, London, W1U 2RN
Email: info@halleonardeurope.com

In Australia, contact:
Hal Leonard Australia Pty. Ltd.
4 Lentara Court
Cheltenham, Victoria, 3192 Australia
Email: info@halleonard.com.au

CAFÉ DE PARIS

To Judy Dye

By EUGÉNIE ROCHEROLLE

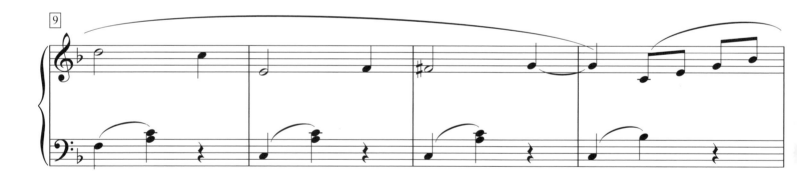

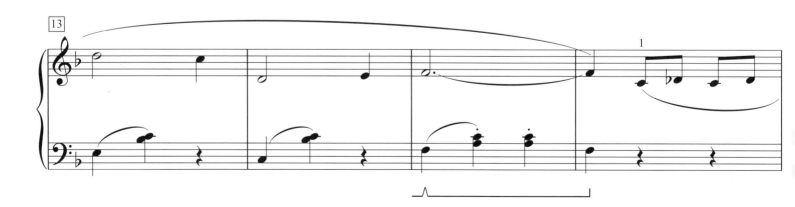

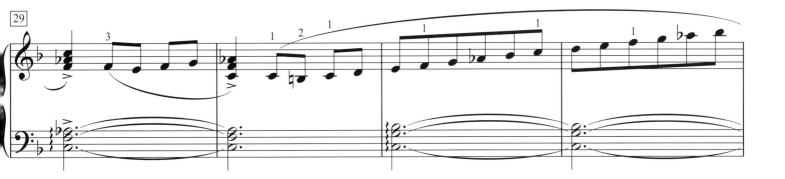

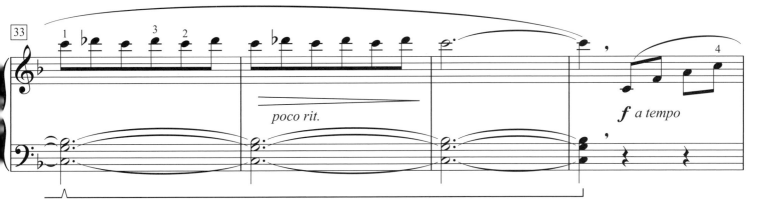

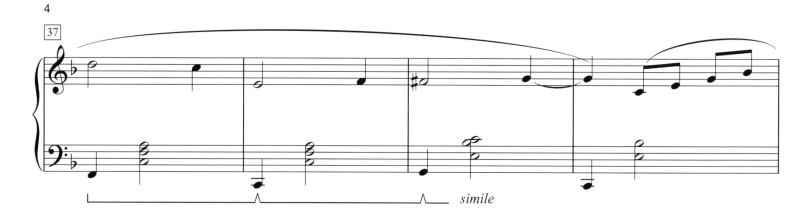

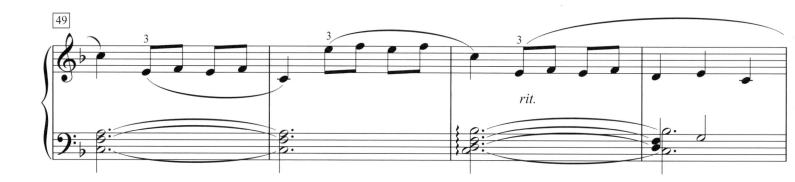

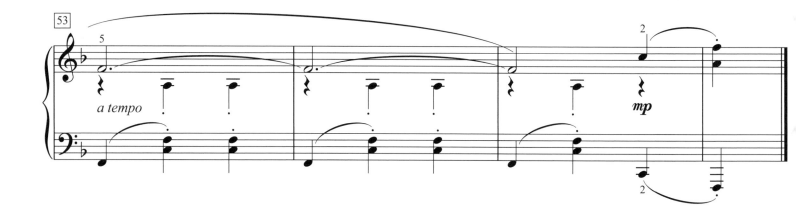

LAST DANCE

To Anya Laurence

By EUGÉNIE ROCHEROLLE

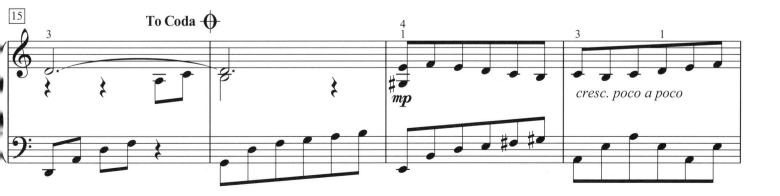

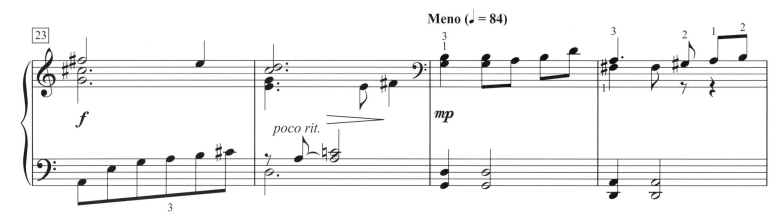

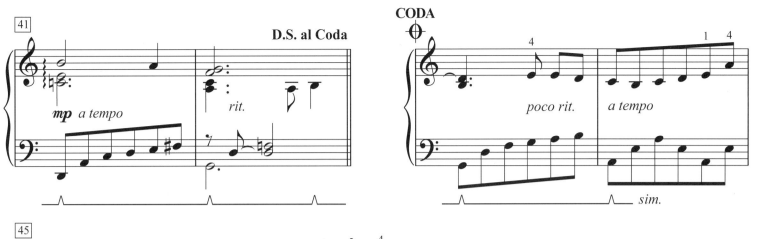

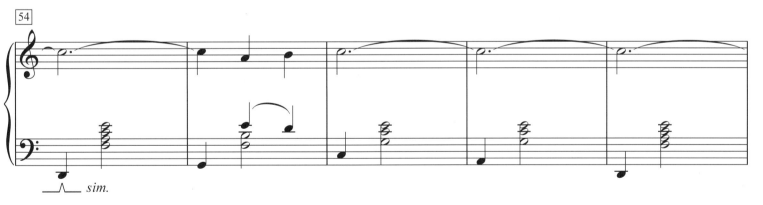

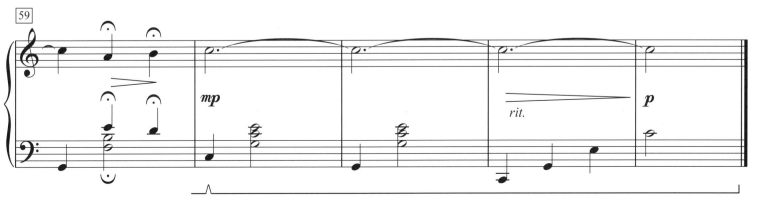

CELEBRACIÓN

To Ernest Kramer

By EUGÉNIE ROCHEROLLE

10

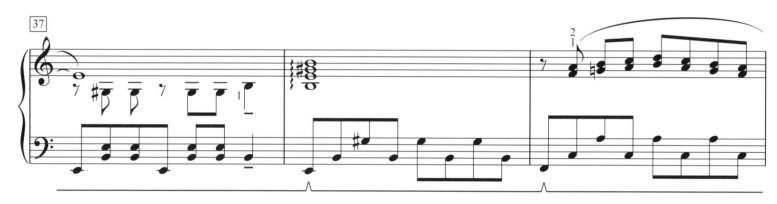

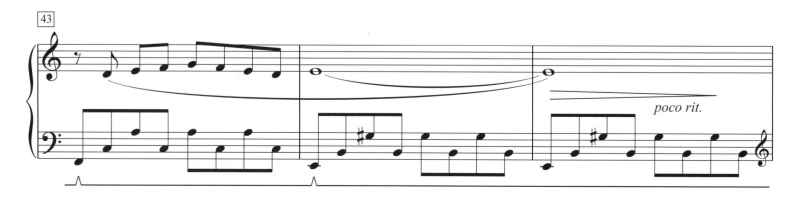

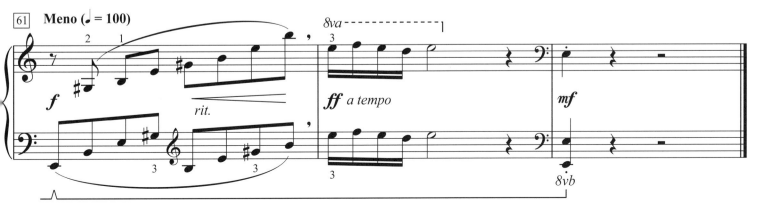

MEMENTO

To Diana Pettit

By EUGÉNIE ROCHEROLLE

Freely, with feeling (♩. = 50)

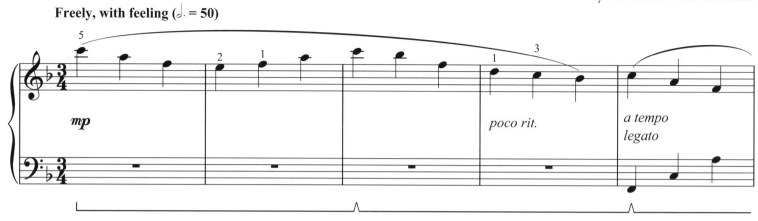

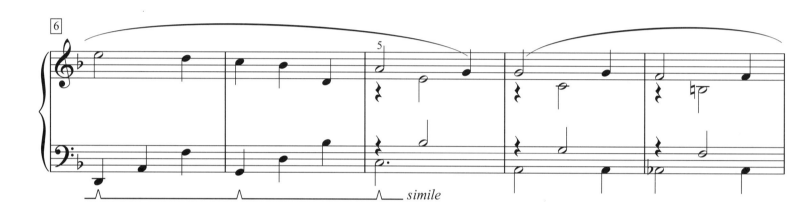

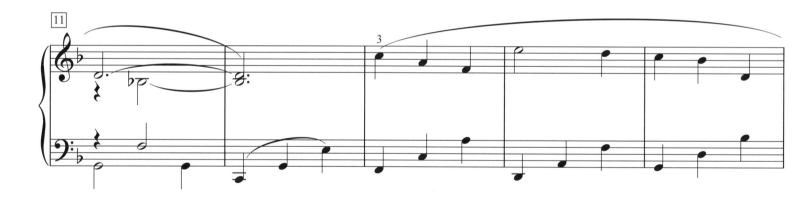

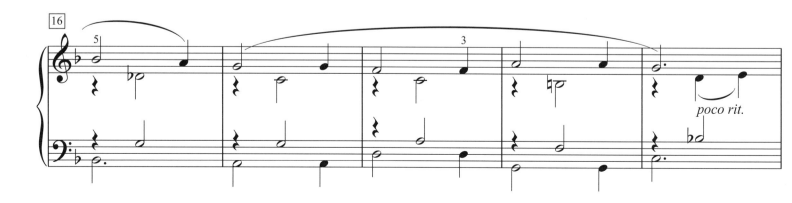

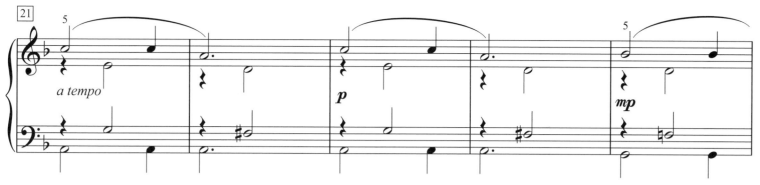

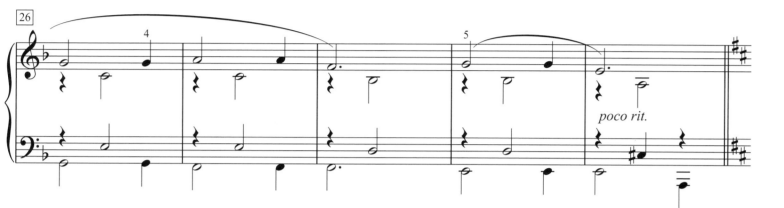

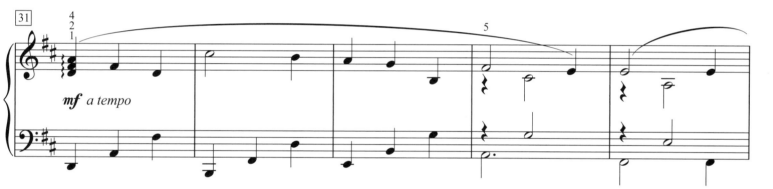

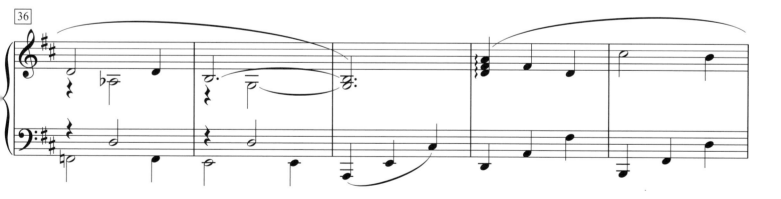

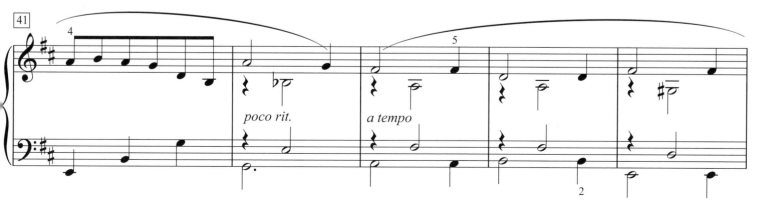

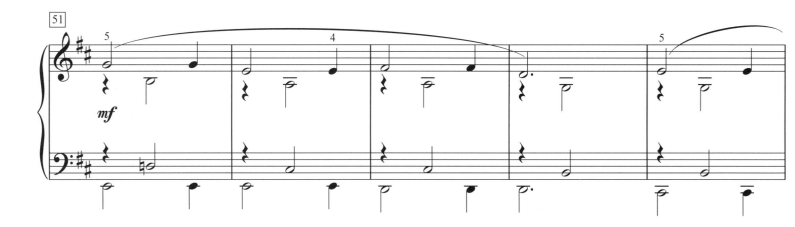

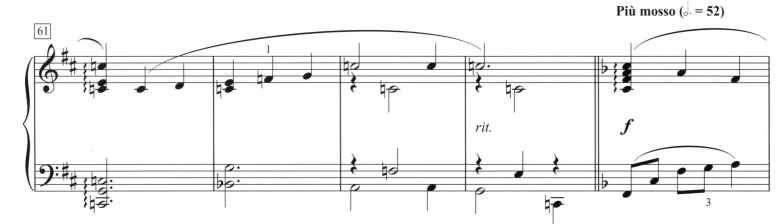

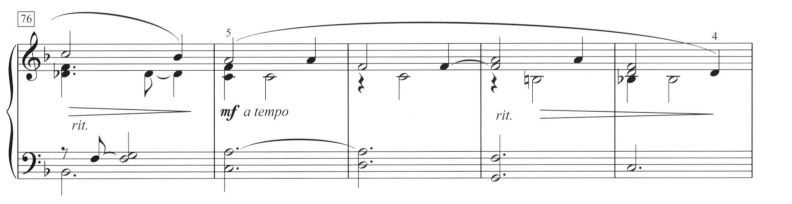

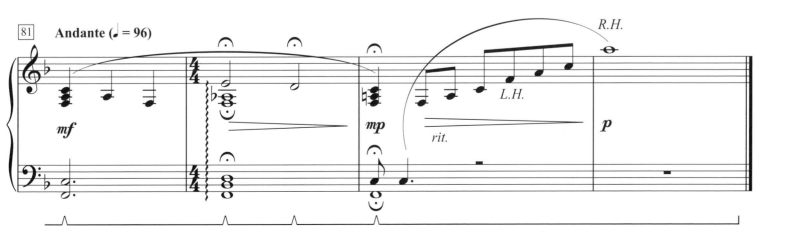

LONGINGS

To Cecelia Wyatt

By EUGÉNIE ROCHEROLLE

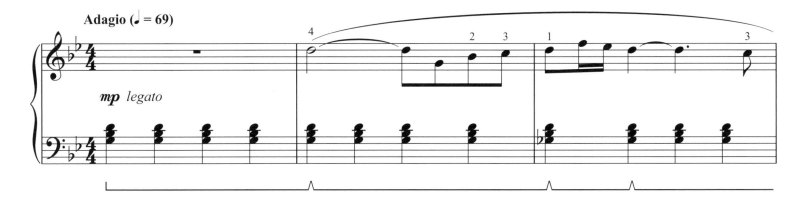

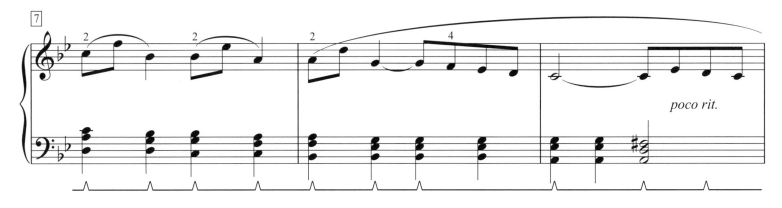

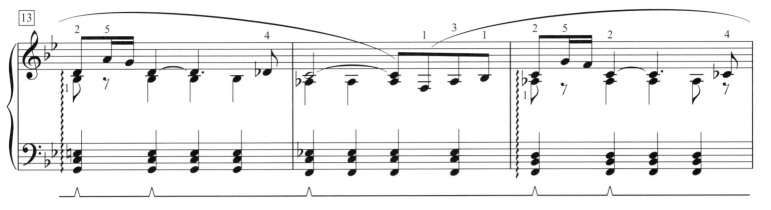

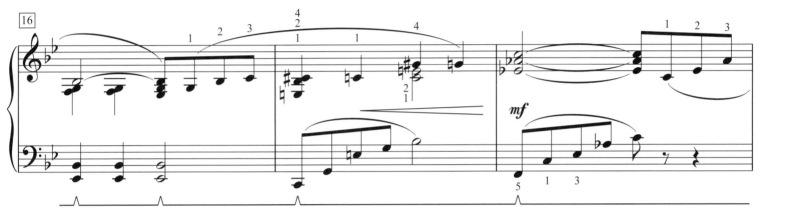

REFLECTIONS

To Millette Alexander

By EUGÉNIE ROCHEROLLE

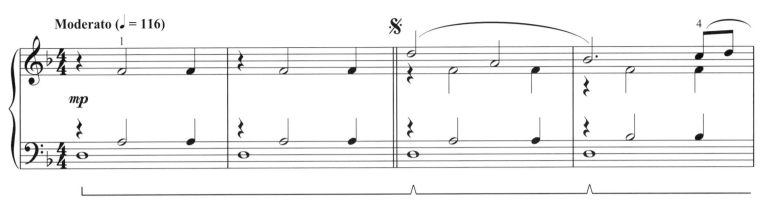

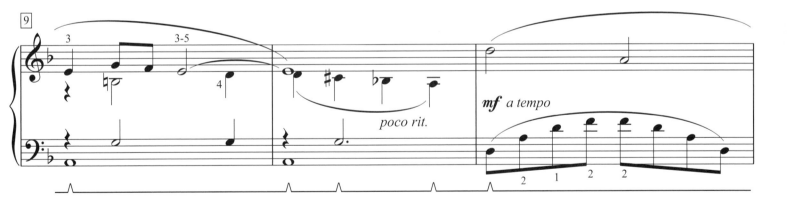

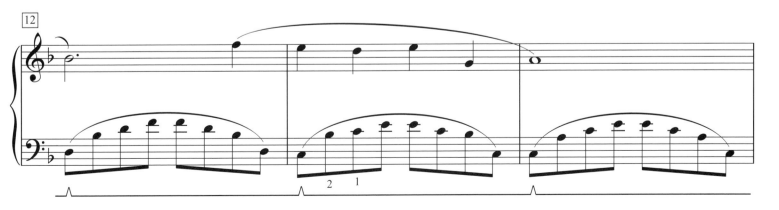

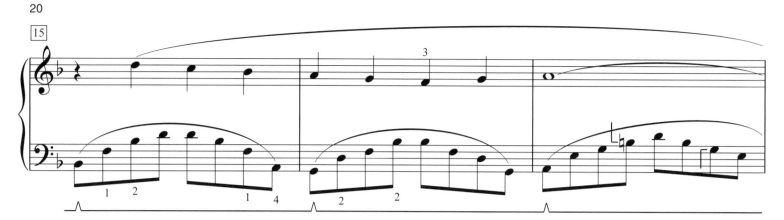

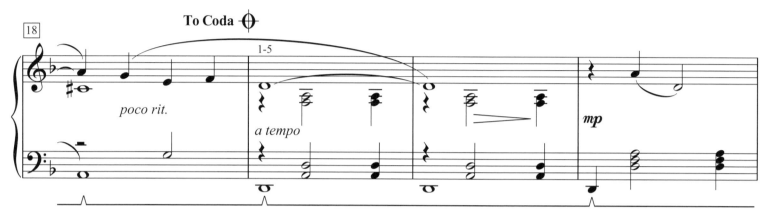

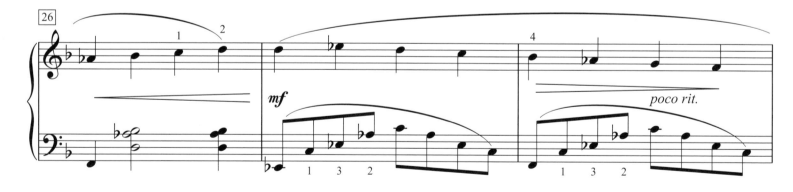

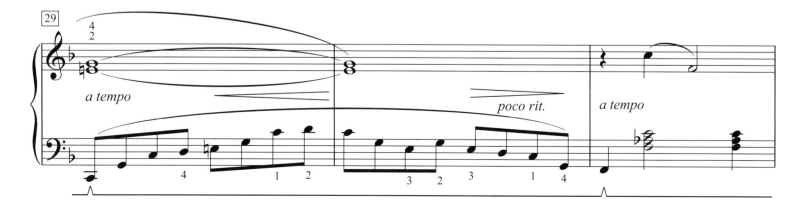

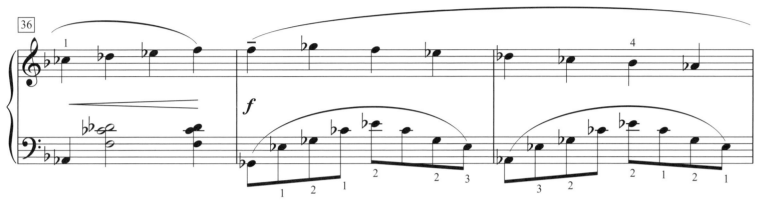

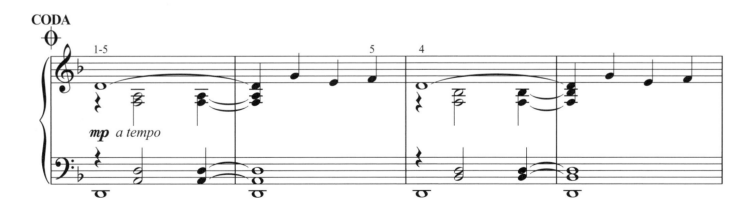

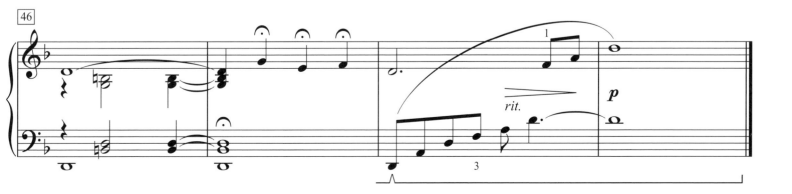

RAPSODIE

To Julie Rivers

By EUGÉNIE ROCHEROLLE

Allegro moderato (♩ = 132)

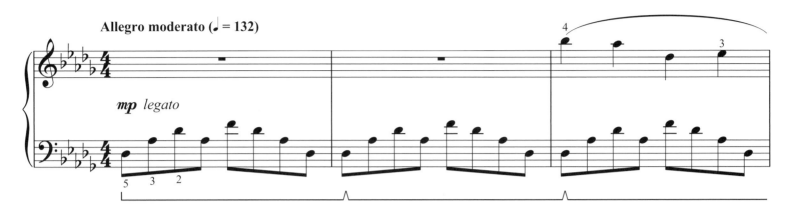

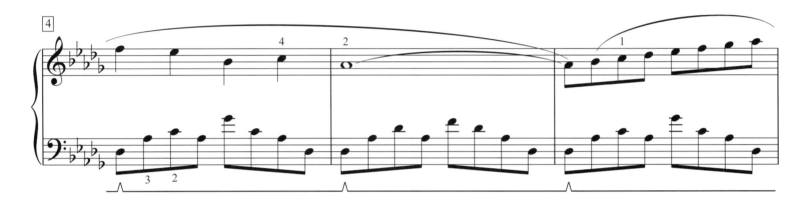

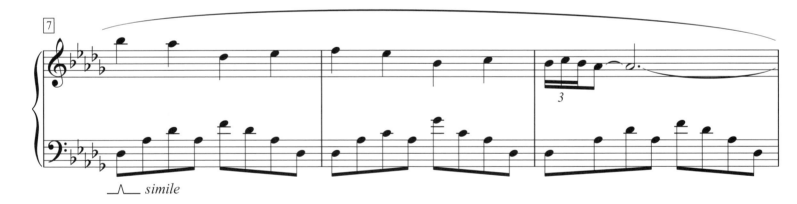

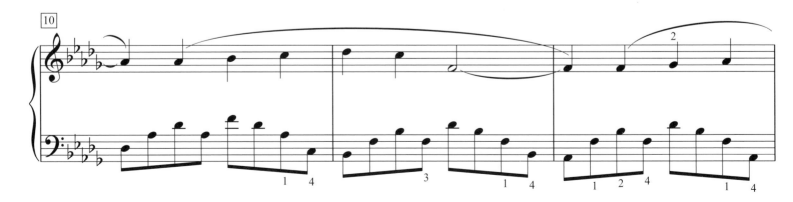

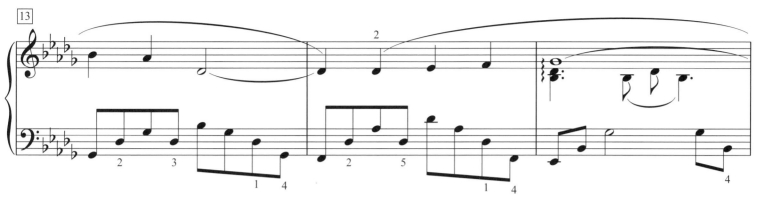

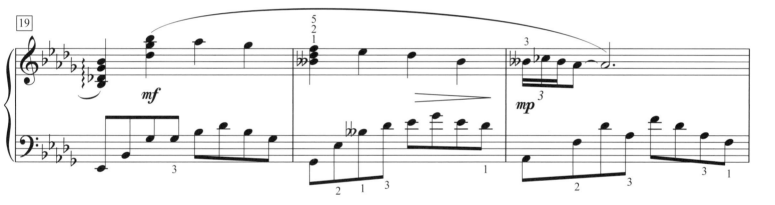

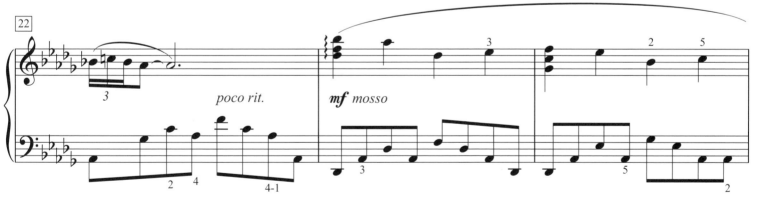

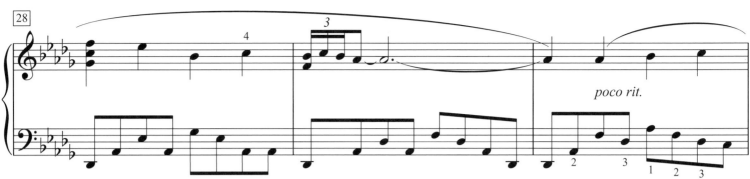

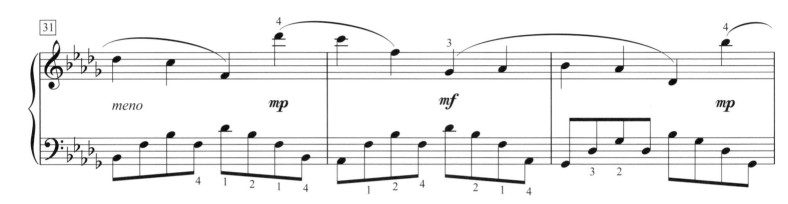

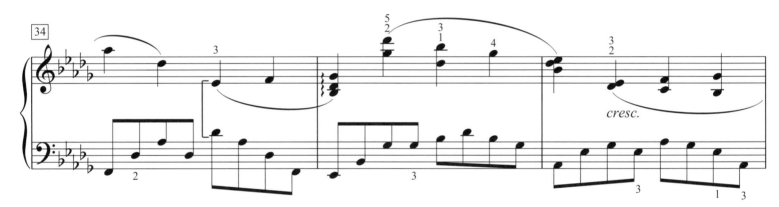

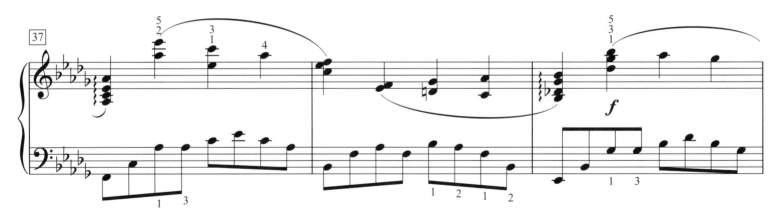

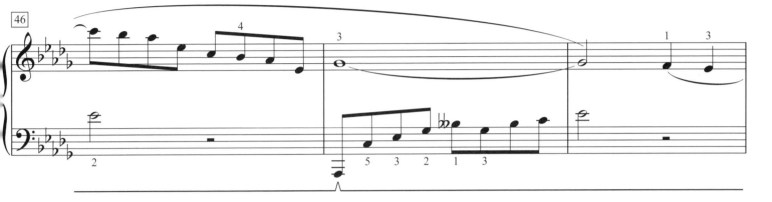

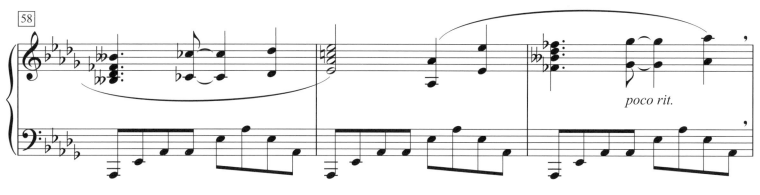

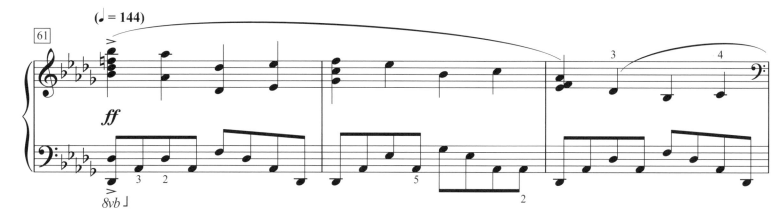

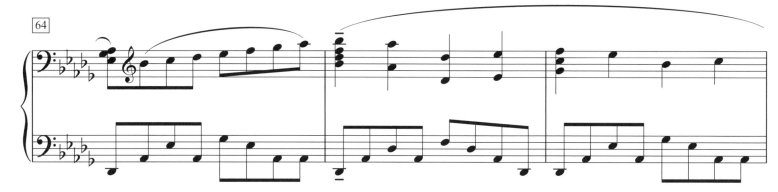

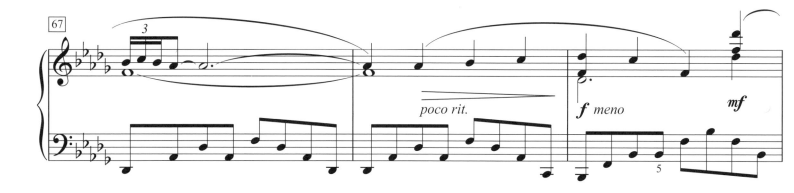

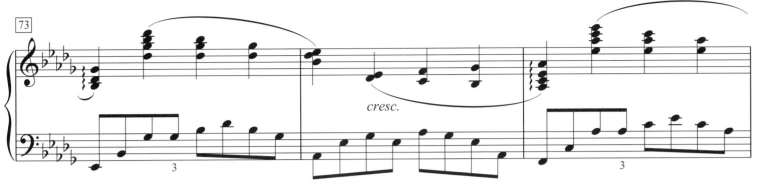

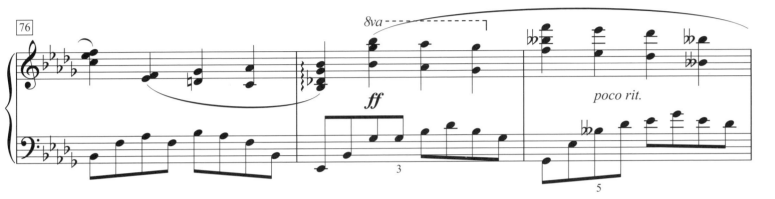

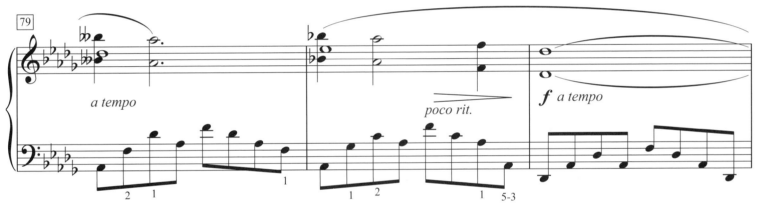

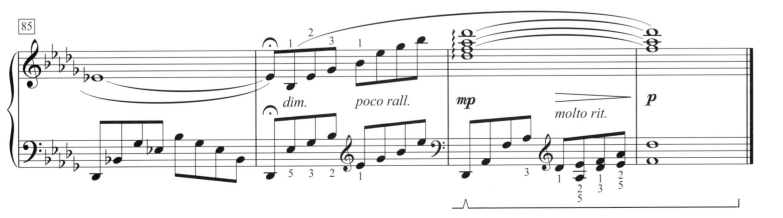

ROMANCE

To Sandra Shaw Murphy

By EUGÉNIE ROCHEROLLE

Moderato (♩ = 112)

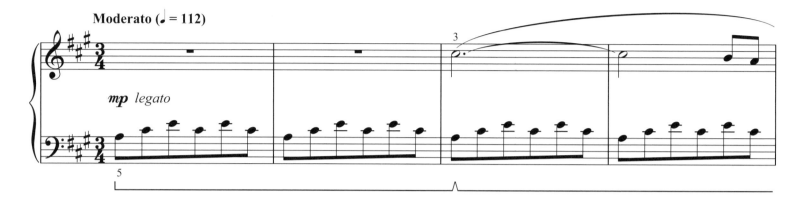

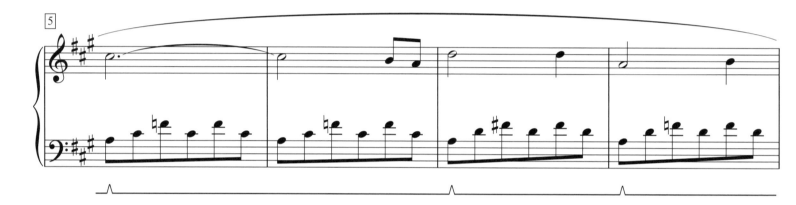

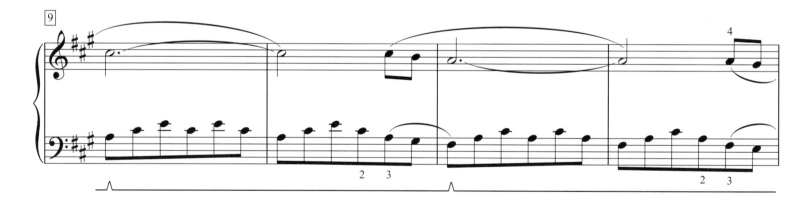

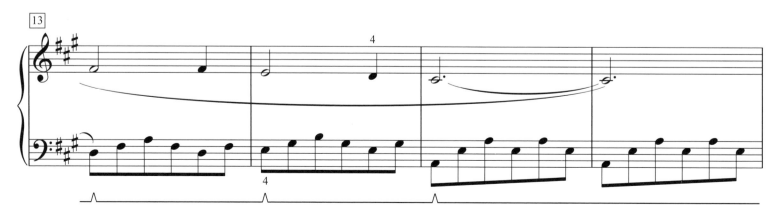

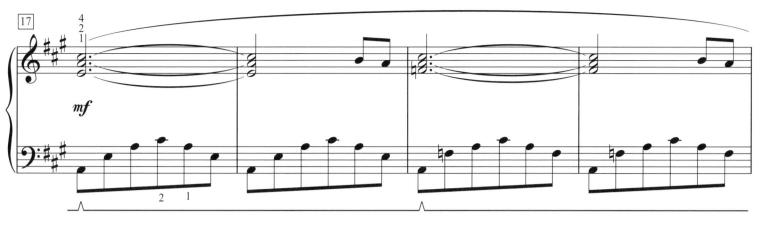

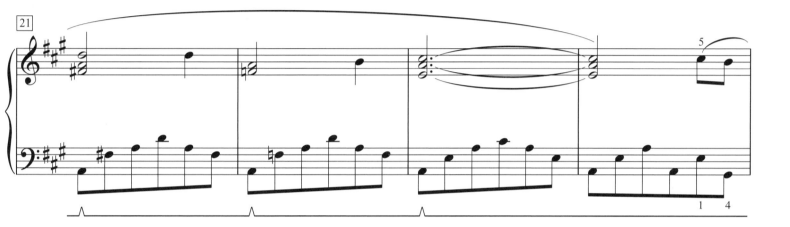

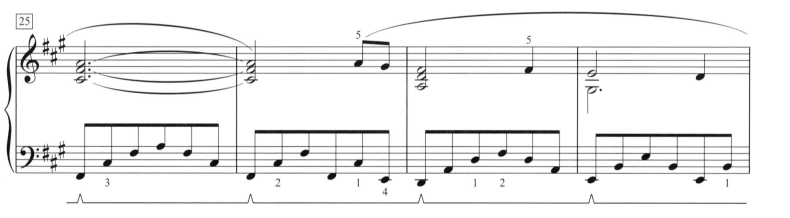

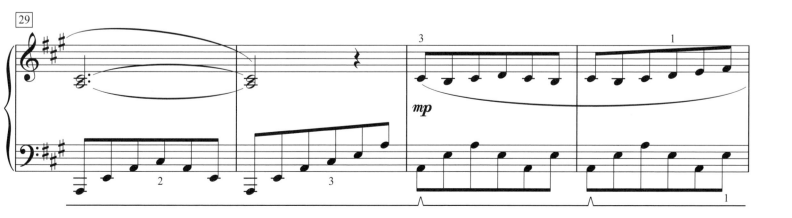

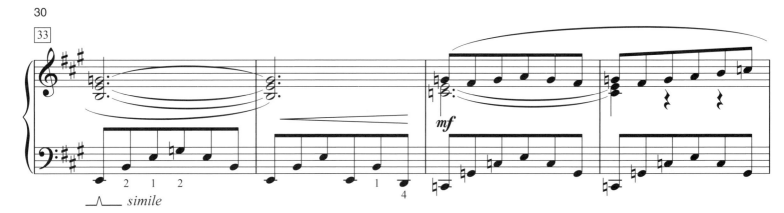

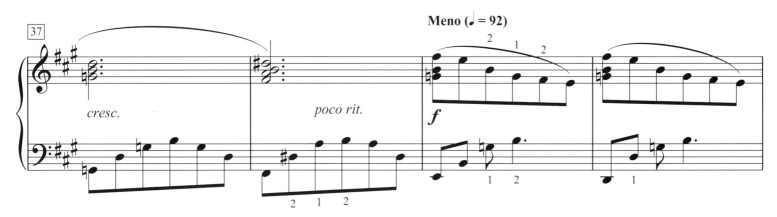

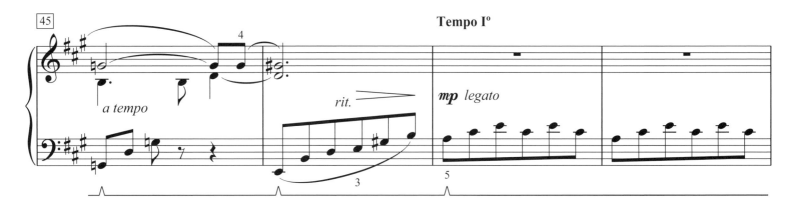

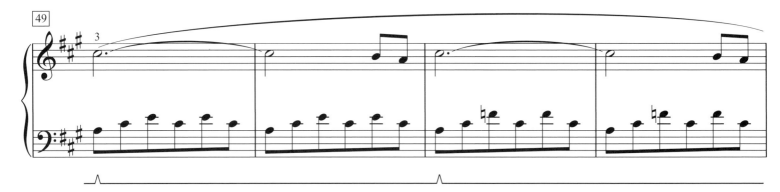

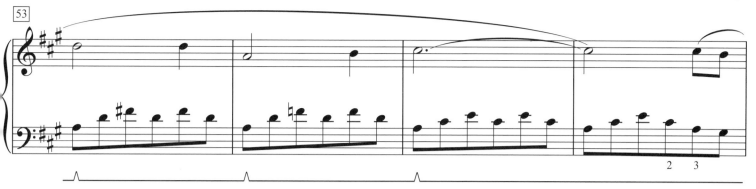

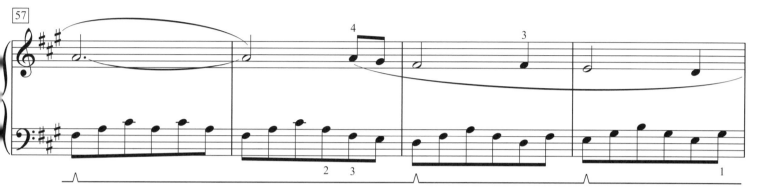

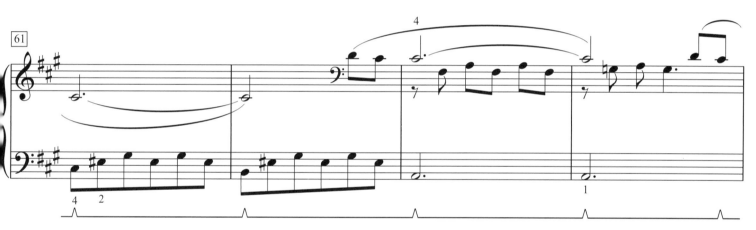

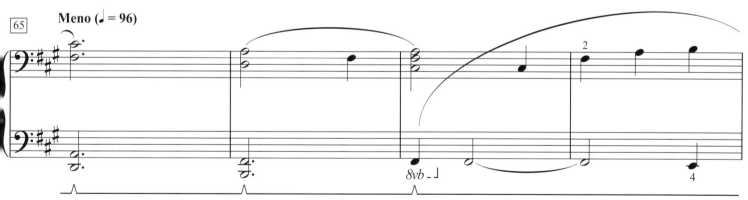

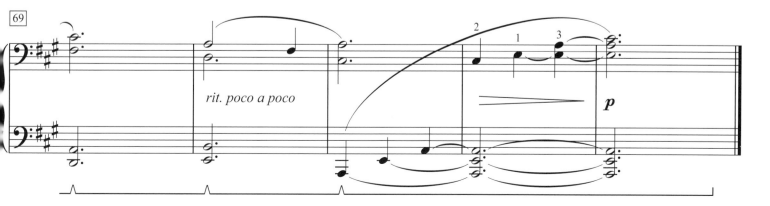

THE EUGÉNIE ROCHEROLLE SERIES

Offering both original compositions and popular arrangements, these stunning collections are ideal for intermediate-level pianists! Many include audio tracks performed by Ms. Rocherolle.

Candlelight Christmas
Eight traditional carols: Away in a Manger • Coventry Carol • Joseph Dearest, Joseph Mine • O Holy Night (duet) • O Little Town of Bethlehem • Silent Night • The Sleep of the Infant Jesus • What Child Is This?
00311808..$14.99

Christmas Together
Six piano duet arrangements: Blue Christmas • The Christmas Song (Chestnuts Roasting on an Open Fire) • Rudolph the Red-Nosed Reindeer • Santa Baby • Up on the Housetop • We Wish You a Merry Christmas.
00102838 ....$14.99

Classic Jazz Standards
Ten beloved tunes: Blue Skies • Georgia on My Mind • Isn't It Romantic? • Lazy River • The Nearness of You • On the Sunny Side of the Street • Stardust • Stormy Weather • and more.
00311424 ....$12.99

Continental Suite
Six original piano solos: Belgian Lace • In Old Vienna • La Piazza • Les Avenues De Paris • Oktoberfest • Rondo Capichio.
00312111 ....$12.99

Fantasia del Tango
Six original piano solos (and a bonus piano duet!): Bailando Conmigo • Debajo las Estrellas • Ojos de Coqueta • Promesa de Amor • Suenos de Ti • Suspiros • Tango Caprichoso.
00199978 ....$12.99

George Gershwin – Three Preludes
Accessible for intermediate-level pianists: Allegro ben ritmato e deciso • Andante con moto e poco rubato • Agitato.
00111939 ....$10.99

It's Me, O Lord
Nine traditional spirituals: Deep River • It's Me, O Lord • Nobody Knows De Trouble I See • Swing Low, Sweet Chariot • and more.
00311368..$12.99

Mancini Classics
Songs: Baby Elephant Walk • Charade • Days of Wine and Roses • Dear Heart • How Soon • Inspector Clouseau Theme • It Had Better Be Tonight • Moment to Moment • Moon River.
00118878 ....$14.99

Meaningful Moments
Eight memorable pieces: Adagio • Bridal March • Elegy • Recessional • Wedding March • Wedding Processional. Plus, arrangements of beloved favorites Amazing Grace and Ave Maria.
00279100 ....$9.99

New Orleans Sketches
Titles: Big Easy Blues • Bourbon Street Beat • Carnival Capers • Jivin' in Jackson Square • Masquerade! • Rex Parade.
00139675..$12.99

On the Jazzy Side
Six original solos. Songs: High Five! • Jubilation! • Prime Time • Small Talk • Small Town Blues • Travelin' Light.
00311982..$12.99

HAL•LEONARD®
www.halleonard.com

Recuerdos Hispanicos
Seven original solos: Brisas Isleñas (Island Breezes) • Dia de Fiesta (Holiday) • Un Amor Quebrado (A Lost Love) • Resonancias de España (Echoes of Spain) • Niña Bonita (Pretty Girl) • Fantasia del Mambo (Mambo Fantasy) • Cuentos del Matador (Tales of the Matador).
00311369..$9.99

Rodgers & Hammerstein Selected Favorites
Eight favorites: Climb Ev'ry Mountain • Do-Re-Mi • If I Loved You • Oklahoma • Shall We Dance? • Some Enchanted Evening • There Is Nothin' like a Dame • You'll Never Walk Alone. Includes a CD of Eugénie performing each song.
00311928..$14.99

Romantic Stylings
Eight original piano solos: Cafe de Paris • Celebracion • Last Dance • Longings • Memento • Rapsodie • Reflections • Romance.
00312272 ....$14.99

Swingin' the Blues
Six blues originals: Back Street Blues • Big Shot Blues • Easy Walkin' Blues • Hometown Blues • Late Night Blues • Two-Way Blues.
00311445..$12.95

Two's Company
Titles: Island Holiday • La Danza • Mood in Blue • Postcript • Whimsical Waltz.
00311883 ....$12.99

Valses Sentimentales
Seven original solos: Bal Masque (Masked Ball) • Jardin de Thé (Tea Garden) • Le Long du Boulevard (Along the Boulevard) • Marché aux Fleurs (Flower Market) • Nuit sans Etoiles (Night Without Stars) • Palais Royale (Royal Palace) • Promenade á Deux (Strolling Together).
00311497..$9.99

0819

439